AN ALASKAN ADVENTURE

For Beverly —E.K-P.

For Josh, Jesse and Erika —K.S.

Library of Congress Cataloging-in-Publication Data
Koehler-Pentacoff, Elizabeth.
John Muir and Stickeen : an Alaskan adventure / by Elizabeth Koehler-Pentacoff ; illustrated by Karl Swanson.
p. cm.
Summary: Describes an episode in the life of conservationist John Muir when he was stranded on a glacier with a brave dog, Stickeen.
ISBN 0-7613-2769-X (lib. bdg.) — ISBN 0-7613-1997-2 (trade)
1. Dogs—Alaska—Anecdotes—Juvenile literature. 2. Muir, John, 1838-1914—Journeys—Alaska—Juvenile literature. 3. Stickeen (Dog)—Juvenile literature. [1. Stickeen (Dog) 2. Dogs. 3. Muir, John, 1838-1914—Journeys—Alaska.] I. Swanson, Karl W. II. Title.
QL795.D6K814 2003
333.7'2'092—dc21
2003002218

Published by
The Millbrook Press, Inc.
2 Old New Milford Road
Brookfield, Connecticut 06804
www.millbrookpress.com

Designed by Tania Garcia
Printed in Hong Kong

5 4 3 2 1 lib.
5 4 3 2 1 trade

John Muir and Stickeen

AN ALASKAN ADVENTURE

BY ELIZABETH KOEHLER-PENTACOFF
ILLUSTRATED BY KARL SWANSON

THE MILLBROOK PRESS • BROOKFIELD, CONNECTICUT

John Muir and Stickeen stand near a glacier in southeast Alaska.

Wind whips the small dog's coat. It blows his fur.

Rain sweeps down in torrents.

"Go back to your tent!" shouts John to Stickeen.

But Stickeen stays by his side. He loves adventure as much as John does.

John sighs and reaches in his pocket for a piece of bread.

They share the meager breakfast beneath a shelter of ice cliffs and trees.

It is the only food they will eat all day.

Mountain streams crash upon boulders. Trees bend in the wind.

John loves the excitement. He enjoys nature's fierce weather.

He tries to draw the scene in his notebook.

But the rain is too wild.

He uses his ax to make steps in the glacier's side.

Step by step John climbs upward. Step by step Stickeen follows.

They reach the top. The rain ceases.

A crystal land stretches for seven miles.

Miles and miles of ice. Miles and miles of cold.

Only John Muir, Stickeen, and the wilderness.

They have all day to explore.

They examine a crevasse. The crack in the ice leads down, down, into vast blackness. John cuts hollows for his feet so he will not slip. He looks at Stickeen. Then he jumps.

With no hesitation, Stickeen follows. John admires the little dog's bravery.

Stickeen belongs to John's friend Samuel. But no one can really own him. Stickeen is cold and aloof. He does not give or want affection. He seems only to like adventure in the wilderness.

They travel on. John studies his compass and plans their course. They must return to camp before dark. Night without shelter would be too cold. Darkness on a glacier filled with crevasses could mean death.

Hours pass. Hunger gnaws at John. The bread he shared with Stickeen this morning was hardly a breakfast.

The rough glacier cuts into the dog's paws. Stickeen leaves a trail of red.

John tears up his handkerchief. Gently, he winds it around Stickeen's paws. Now the dog has "moccasins" to protect him from the rough ice.

Stickeen trots onward, ready for adventure.

The sky darkens. The storm's music begins.

Wind gusts the snow. John and Stickeen see only a blur of white.

With every step they face danger.

With every step they face death.

Freezing. Hungry. Wet.

A chasm of blackness stretches eight feet in front of them.

"We can jump it, my boy," shouts John over the wind.

John can see that the ice is lower on the other side. They can make the jump. But they would never be able to retrace their steps.

Should they go back the way they came? Miles and miles.

Too far to turn back now. Night will come soon.

It would be easier to complete their circle on the glacier, rather than go back the way they came. They must go on.

The ice beyond the chasm looks stable and inviting.

John decides to go forward. He runs and leaps. He flies over the edge of darkness and lands on the other side.

Stickeen sails over the crevasse to join him.

For a moment they rest.

The wind wails over the prairie of ice. There is no turning back now. They will circle back to their campsite.

Carefully, John and Stickeen grope their way across the glacier. Wind gusts the snow. They are on an ice island, separated by crevasses.

In front of them lies the largest crevasse they could imagine. It is fifty feet wide.

John studies the gap. Only a thin ice bridge spans the gaping hole.

How will they cross? And if they fall?

Stickeen whines.

"Don't worry," says John aloud. The wind sweeps his voice away with the snow.

"At worst we can only slip, and then how grand a grave we will have."

The ice bridge flows downward. Razor thin near the center.

John knows what they must do. They must scale down this side of the glacier to reach the bridge. Somehow, they must cross the bridge and get to the ledge on the other side. If they make it to the ledge, they will have to climb straight up to the top.

John leans over. Snow crusts his eyelashes.

His frozen fingers hold the ax. The ax cuts a curve for his knees. He works carefully. Slowly. He must not slip. He is only inches away from death.

Stickeen cries. Paces. Paws the ice. They look into each other's eyes.

"Yes, Stickeen," says John. "This is the only way."

They can't retrace their steps. They must get back before dark.

John kneels. He cuts steps on the wall below for his feet.

Every stroke is a dance with death.

Stickeen runs back and forth, searching for another way. He moans, as if begging John not to cross.

John slides his leg down the sheer ridge. His foot finds the step.

Crouching, his left hand in a groove, he cuts more notches.

Blasts of wind try to pull him into the chasm.

Inch by inch, John creeps down to the bridge. Balancing on the last step, he bends to ride the edge.

His knees grip the ice. He flattens the sharp edge with his ax. This makes the bridge wider for Stickeen to cross. John inches forward until he reaches the other wall.

Stickeen's cries get louder and louder. He runs back and forth along the edge.

Again, John makes a ladder. Up, up, he climbs. Up to the top of the cliff.

The wind draws out Stickeen's yelps.

"You can do it, my boy," shouts John.

Stickeen wails. But does not cross.

What should John do now? Darkness approaches. They must get off the glacier while they can still see.

He pretends to leave. John walks away, hoping Stickeen will start his journey. Instead, the dog lies down and sobs.

John walks to the edge. "Come on," he yells.

At last Stickeen rises. He crouches into the hollow John has made. He stares into the first step.

He slides his paws together over the edge. He molds his body into the rung.

Down the ice ladder until he reaches the ledge. Then, with a measured rhythm, he creeps across to the bottom of the other side.

What now? John wonders if he should make a noose out of his clothes to haul the dog up.

Stickeen stares, as if in a trance.

Suddenly, he springs forward, paws flying up the ladder.

In one brief, glorious moment, the terrier leaps past the edge and rushes into the wind.

Past John. Into safety.

John tries to pet Stickeen. But Stickeen will not be still.

He runs in circles, dashes here and there. He pants. He barks. Rolling over and over, he yelps and darts this way and that.

Finally, his racing slows to a trot and he joins John to journey toward their camp in the mountains.

Two miles to go. They make their way off the glacier.

On land, they stumble through brush and logs. Tired but exhilarated, they push on.

As darkness falls, the sound of gunshots guides them back to camp.

Before the fire John recounts their tale.

Stickeen lays his head on Muir's knee.

Survivors.

About John Muir

❖❖❖❖

John Muir was born in Scotland on April 21, 1838. He grew up in a big family, with four sisters and two brothers. When he was eleven, they moved to a farm in Wisconsin. Life on the farm meant hard work for everyone. They would start their days at 4:00 A.M. doing farm chores. John helped milk the cows, chop firewood, and hoe fields.

Once in a while, on Sunday afternoons, the children had free time. John read James Audubon's stories about North American birds. He searched for birds and their nests in meadows. This began his lifelong love of nature.

As an adult, he explored the wilderness. John wrote what he saw and thought in journals about his travels. He drew pictures and recorded temperatures. John collected plants and followed animal tracks. He analyzed the Earth's surface to learn how the Earth was formed.

Often John walked 25 miles (40 km) a day. Most people would seek shelter during storms, but this is when John often began his journeys. Once during a windstorm, he climbed a 100-foot (30-m) fir tree and sat there for hours. The wind ripped other trees out of the earth. His tree bent nearly to the ground. But John enjoyed experiencing nature's sounds, smells, and sights during the gale.

This story is about his favorite adventure. He traveled to Alaska in 1880 with his friend the Reverend Samuel Young, Young's dog, Stickeen, and several Stickeen Indians. One morning when everyone else still slept, John and Stickeen left their camp to explore a glacier.

An explorer, naturalist, and writer, John Muir became famous for his knowledge of glaciers. He helped to establish Yosemite and Sequoia National Parks. John convinced President Theodore Roosevelt to preserve 148 million acres (6 million hectares) of forest. As founder of the Sierra Club in 1892, John Muir did much to help our environment.

John wrote about his Alaskan adventure in his book, *Stickeen*.

Someone stole Stickeen from the Reverend Young in 1883. Although no one knows what became of the little dog, we do know that he changed people's opinions about animals. During the nineteenth century, people thought animals lacked intelligence and passion. Stickeen proved them wrong.